A JUNKYARD ADVENTURE

GIANT of GEOGRAPHY

Tevin Hansen

Handersen Publishing, LLC
Lincoln, Nebraska

Meet Uncle Larry

The junk store on Broadway Street had a million things for sale. And the man who owned the shop had a million stories to tell.

His name was Uncle Larry.

The sign out front...

Uncle Larry's Antique Shop

...wasn't a complete lie.

There really were antiques inside his store. There were old lamps, paintings with fancy wood frames, art sculptures, baseball and hockey cards, jewelry and furniture, old collectible toys, and lots of other things.

The junkyard was out back.

Uncle Larry had a bunch of junky old cars and smashed-up trucks that would cost so much to fix that it was cheaper to buy a new car.

Uncle Larry's store also had some of the coolest stuff on the planet. Decades worth of junk and antiques were packed, racked, and stacked into his crowded old shop on Broadway. His apartment was just above the store.

Uncle Larry was a friendly old man who loved to sell things and talk to people. He never married, and never had any children, but he loved to tell stories to kids while their parents shopped in his store.

If it was okay with their moms or dads, or whoever the kids were out shopping with, Uncle Larry would grab his old brown leather stool, plunk right down in the middle of the store, and tell a story.

Uncle Larry had a million stories to tell.

And they always came true.

1
New
Neighbor

After school each day, Eli and Grace had to wait an hour for Dad to get home from work. He had started his new job as a computer programmer, which kept him busy all week.

Jocelyn, the new neighbor girl, would come over and watch them until Dad got home, usually a little before 5:00 p.m.

Today they were doing some research on Dad's computer. They were learning all about decorations they could buy for their new fish tank.

"Ooh, I like that one," said Grace, as she pointed to the screen.

"The gray castle?" asked Eli.

"No, not that one," said Grace, smacking his hand away. "*That* one, right there. The pink one, with all the heart shapes."

Eli shook his head. "Forget it!"

"Why?" asked Grace. "What's wrong with it?"

Jocelyn laughed. "What about the fish?" she asked, sitting right beside them. "You two have spent all this time looking at decorations for the fish tank, but you don't even have any fish yet."

Eli scratched his chin. "Good point."

"We'll ask Dad," said Grace.

"Yeah, whenever he gets home," said Eli. "I wonder what's taking him so long?"

It was already 4:40 p.m.

Before they had a chance to research some fish that might look good swimming around their new aquarium, they heard keys jiggling in the lock. The front door opened and in came Dad.

The time was 4:42.

"Hi, Dad," said Eli.

"Daddy!" Grace raced over and gave him a huge hug before he even shut the door.

"Hi, Mr. Fernandez," said Jocelyn.

"Hi, Jocelyn," said Dad. "How did it go?"

"Oh, they were fine," said Jocelyn. "They did their homework, ate some cereal, and then we were researching decorations for your new aquarium."

"Yeah, speaking of decorations..." Eli rubbed his hands together. "Can we go to Uncle Larry's now?"

"Pleeeease?" said Grace. "You promised."

Dad dropped his laptop bag and car keys down on the counter. "I did promise, didn't I?"

Eli and Grace nodded.

"You told us we had to wait until after school on Friday," Grace reminded him.

"And today's Friday," said Eli.

Dad sighed. Then he picked up the car keys from off the counter. "How about you, Jocelyn? Do you want to come too?"

Eli and Grace's eyes lit up.

Jocelyn shook her head. "Sorry, guys, I can't. I promised my mom we would make dinner tonight. Then we're supposed to call my grandma, since she's been so sick. Plus I've got swimming practice at six a.m. tomorrow morning."

Eli and Grace both looked disappointed.

"Next time, okay?" said Jocelyn.

Grace looked the most upset. "Okay," she said. "But you have to promise you'll come with us when Dad takes us to Uncle Larry's."

"I promise," said Jocelyn.

"Pinky Promise?" said Grace, and she held out her pinky for Jocelyn to grab onto.

"Pinky promise," said Jocelyn, then wrapped her pinky around Grace's small finger.

Eli and Grace had let the new neighbor girl in on their secret. They told Jocelyn all about their junkyard adventures, and what a great time they'd been having at Uncle Larry's magical store.

Jocelyn didn't believe their wild stories, but she was still curious about going with them.

Dad paid Jocelyn her babysitting money for the week, then they all headed outside. Eli and Grace were already buckled, ready to go.

Dad started the car. Then he rolled down his window to shout, "Have a good night, Jocelyn. Say hi to your mother for me!"

"I will!" shouted Jocelyn, as she headed home. "Bye, Eli! Bye, Grace! Have fun on your adventure!"

"We will!" they shouted from the back seat.

As soon as Dad pulled out of the driveway and started heading down the street, he looked at the clock and said, "Uh-oh."

"What's wrong?" asked Eli.

"Looks like we'd better hurry," said Dad, making a left turn.

"Why, Dad?" asked Grace.

"Well, it's already 4:45, and Uncle Larry's store closes at 5:30," said Dad. "It takes about thirty minutes to get there, depending on how bad traffic is."

Eli and Grace spent the whole car ride worrying that there wouldn't be enough time for a junkyard adventure.

2
Unlikely Adventure

When they arrived at Uncle Larry's Antique Shop & Junkyard, the time was 5:15 p.m. That only left fifteen minutes until the store closed.

Eli and Grace wouldn't have much time to pick out decorations for the aquarium. Which also meant there wouldn't be enough time left over for one of Uncle Larry's magical adventures.

Dad had to search for a place to park because the parking lot was so full of vehicles.

"Wow," said Dad. "Uncle Larry must be having a sale today. Look at all these cars!" He found an empty spot, then the whole family headed inside.

"Hi, Larry!" said Dad, waving at the owner.

Uncle Larry waved back. But he was busy dealing with last-minute customers, so he didn't have much time to talk when he came over.

"Eli! Grace! How are you?" said Uncle Larry with a big wave and an even bigger smile.

Eli and Grace smiled back.

"We're going to buy decorations for our new aquarium," said Grace.

"Wonderful!" said Uncle Larry, sounding very excited about fish tank decorations. He put a finger to his stubbly chin and said, "Fish tank, fish tank...hmm. I believe all the new aquarium decorations are over in aisle two. No, wait—"

"Aisle *three*," said another voice.

Uncle Larry jumped. "Oh, there you are," he said, speaking to the man who startled him.

The man was taller than their dad, who was quite tall. He wore an old gray sweater that matched his scruffy gray beard.

"Folks, I'd like you to meet a dear old friend of mine," said Uncle Larry. "This is, um...Mr. Harvard."

The man smiled. "Mr. Harvard, or Professor

12

Harvard, or Doctor Harvard..." He raised his hands and shrugged his shoulders. "Any one of those is fine. Lately, my students have taken to calling me Professor H, or even Professor H-dawg," he said with a laugh.

Dad and Professor Harvard shook hands. Eli and Grace couldn't help but notice how hairy the man's hands were—hairy like a dog's paws.

"And you must be Ben," said Professor Harvard.

"Yes," said Dad. "And these are—"

"Eli and Grace," said Professor Harvard. "Yes, Uncle Larry has told me all about you two."

While Dad and Professor Harvard chatted for a minute, Eli and Grace spoke in quiet voices to each other. Mostly they were upset because there was no time for a junkyard adventure.

"Is that okay with you two?" asked Dad, staring at them and waiting for an answer.

Neither Eli or Grace had heard the question.

"Um, is what okay, Dad?" said Eli.

Dad messed up Eli's hair. "I *said*...while I look around the store, is it okay if Professor Harvard tells you two a story? The store closes in a few minutes, so it will have to be a fast story, okay?"

Eli and Grace tried not to look too excited. They hadn't told Dad about the magical adventures that happened at Uncle Larry's store. But it seemed that Professor Harvard also knew about this little secret.

"But first—" Professor Harvard leaned down to face them. "First, I believe you two have some decorations to pick out, hm?"

Eli and Grace both agreed.

"Yes, aisle two," said Uncle Larry, then smacked his forehead. "*Three!* I meant, aisle three..." Then he was off to deal with more customers.

"Don't leave the store, okay?" said Dad, as he walked off to do some shopping.

"Okay, Dad!" said Grace.

"We won't!" said Eli.

"When you've made your choices," hollered Dad, "just put them on the counter, okay?"

"We will!" said Eli and Grace.

Dad headed down aisle six. Eli and Grace

were left with Professor Harvard. Neither one of them wanted to be rude, but they were both thinking the same thing: that Professor Harvard looked an awful lot like Uncle Larry's dog, who was probably sleeping somewhere.

"Eli? Grace? Right this way," said Professor Harvard. He led them over to aisle three, where all the fish tank decorations were. But right as he was about to say something, a customer came up and started asking questions.

"Excuse me a moment," said Professor Harvard to Eli and Grace. "I must assist this gentleman who is inquiring about the antique wristwatch."

Eli and Grace were left alone. But that was okay, since they had shopping to do.

"Come on, Grace," said Eli, taking his sister by the hand. "I guess we don't have time for an adventure, after all. But at least we get to pick out some cool new stuff for the fish tank."

3
Big Shoes

Eli and Grace spent the next ten minutes choosing decorations for their new aquarium. Some really tough choices had to be made.

"Red and gold? Or green and blue?" asked Eli. He held up two different fish castles.

"Hmm, I can't decide," said Grace. "I like them both." Actually, she liked all the new decorations that Uncle Larry had for sale. They were going to have the coolest aquarium ever.

When they finally made their choices, Eli and Grace carried them over to the checkout counter.

Uncle Larry was talking to a group of customers over by a cluttered table. The table was loaded with antiques, collectibles, and lots of junk. He'd been dealing with so many customers all day that his hair stood up at funny angles. But he was still smiling, and still happy to talk to each and every customer shopping in his store.

Eli and Grace waited patiently for their dad to finish his shopping.

They waited, and waited.

Sitting on top of the checkout counter was an antique mantel clock with a $25.00 price tag. Written underneath was **O.B.O.**, which they'd learned on their first visit stood for: Or Best Offer.

The clock read 5:29 p.m.

"Only one more minute till closing," said Eli.

"Where's Dad?" asked Grace, as she looked around the store. She was surprised to see so many customers shopping, even though Uncle Larry's store closed in less than a minute.

"I don't know," said Eli, then he pointed. "But there's Mr. Harvard."

"*Professor* Harvard," Grace reminded him. She waved, but didn't think the Professor saw her.

Ding! Ding! Ding!

Rrrrrr-rrrrr...clunk.

Eli and Grace both laughed at the funny sound the old clock made. Although it was scratched up a bit, and sounded funny when it chimed, Uncle Larry's old clock still kept excellent time.

It was now 5:30 p.m.

When Eli and Grace looked around the store, Professor Harvard was walking toward them.

"I see you've made some excellent choices," said Professor Harvard. "I like the silk plants you chose, Grace. I think the fish will like them too."

"Thanks," said Grace.

"I think they will add a nice touch to Eli's choice," said Professor Harvard. "The castle."

Eli said, "You like it?"

"Yes, I do, Eli," said Professor Harvard. "That is an eco-friendly fish castle with a drawbridge, turrets, and lots of open windows for the fish to swim through. And let's not forget—"

Professor Harvard stopped.

"Why the sad face, Eli?" he asked. "You too,

Grace. Is there something bothering you?"

Eli looked at Grace, but neither of them wanted to say too much in front of Uncle Larry's friend. After all, it was Uncle Larry who told them stories and sent them on their junkyard adventures.

"Oh, nothing," said Eli. "It's just that we've gone on some..." He shuffled his feet. "Some really fun adventures here in Uncle Larry's store."

Professor Harvard's bushy gray eyebrows raised up. "You don't say? Well..." He tugged on his beard. "I just so happen to have a few *magic* items right here."

From his pocket, Professor Harvard took out a few small objects. These were the items they would need for their junkyard adventure.

Eli was given a used bottle cap.

Grace was given an old postcard.

Professor Harvard then handed each of them a bandanna, one green and one white.

"There you go!" said Professor Harvard. "I believe you now have everything you need for your next adventure. You know the way..."

Eli and Grace could not have looked happier.

"You mean—?" Eli was shocked. It turns out that Uncle Larry was not the only one that knew about the magic of Uncle Larry's store.

"Yes, Eli, that is exactly what I mean," said Professor Harvard. He winked at both of them. "You'd better hurry, before your father finishes his shopping. I'll go tell him you two need a few more minutes to choose your decorations. Deal?"

Eli and Grace both said, "Deal."

"Off you go!" said Professor Harvard, as he walked away. Over his shoulder, he hollered, "Say hi to Omar for me!"

And without another word of explanation, Professor Harvard went to help Uncle Larry with all the remaining customers.

Eli and Grace could hardly contain their excitement. Still holding on to their 'magic' items, they hurried to the back of the store, right to the door with the familiar **Junkyard Adventures** sign.

As soon as they opened the door, it looked as if their adventure might not happen after all.

The exit was blocked.

"What is *that*?" asked Grace.

"It looks like a..." Eli turned his head sideways. "Hmm." The closer he looked at the object, the more it confused him.

Something very large was blocking the door to the junkyard. No matter which way they turned their heads, they both saw the same shape.

A giant shoe.

4
Pocket View

"Do we climb up on it?" asked Grace.

"I guess so," said Eli. "We'd better hurry, since we don't have much time."

Eli started to climb.

"Wait for me!" said Grace, then followed her brother. There were lots of cracks and grooves to hold onto, so climbing up was easy.

Eli made it to the top, then reached down to help Grace onto the strange object.

"Thanks," said Grace.

"You're welcome," said Eli. "Whoa!" He nearly fell down when the object blocking the door suddenly began to *move*, taking them with it.

"Eli!" shouted Grace. "Help!"

His sister was about to fall.

Eli dove onto his stomach and reached out his arm. He grabbed hold of Grace just before she went sliding over the edge.

"I've got you!" shouted Eli, and held on tight. She wouldn't have fallen very far, but it was still scary for both of them.

Ka-thump!

The object they were riding suddenly smashed down on the ground. The impact sent Eli and Grace tumbling backwards. Not only that, but the heavy thump kicked up a bunch of dust from the junkyard, making them both cough.

"You okay?" asked Eli.

"Yeah, fine," said Grace. "I think..."

Through the cloud of dust, Eli spotted something they could use to climb down.

A rope.

"Wait a second..." Eli looked again.

No, not rope.

Shoelaces.

Before either of them had a chance to climb down, a hand came reaching out for them.

A giant hand.

Four huge fingers and a giant thumb, each as thick as a tree, reached down and scooped up Eli and Grace. The huge hand raised them up, up, and up some more...

Right toward the giant's mouth.

"NO!" shouted Eli.

"Please don't eat us!" shouted Grace.

The giant raised its eyebrows.

"I don't *eat* people," said the giant. "I happen to be a vegetarian."

Eli and Grace were both shocked.

"You're Eli, right?" asked the giant.

"Um, maybe," said Eli.

"And you're Grace, right?"

Grace pretended she didn't know the answer, either. Neither of them wanted to say too much. They still weren't sure if this was a nice giant or a mean giant, like the ones they'd read about in the book of old fairy tales that Dad had at home.

"Well, kids? Here's the deal," said the giant. "Professor H told me we've only got about ten minutes to look around, so..."

"So what, exactly?" asked Eli. He was hoping the giant wasn't going to say it was lunch time.

Grace looked worried too.

"Let's go!" said the giant.

Without any further explanation, the giant pulled open his shirt pocket, about to drop the two tiny humans inside.

"Hey!" shouted Eli. "Where are you–"

Plop!

"–taking us?" Eli was suddenly upside-down at the bottom of the giant's pocket. And worse, Grace came crashing down on top of him.

"Ow! Get off me!" shouted Eli. "Get your stinky feet out of my face!"

"Sorry!" Grace tried to wiggle her way back to a standing position. She was much more flexible than her older brother, so she got to her feet first.

"Eli, get up here!" shouted Grace. "You can see everything!"

Eli finally managed to stand up beside Grace. Now they were both able to see over the top of the giant's shirt pocket.

The two of them—*three*, including the giant—were traveling at a great speed.

The steady noise...

Swoosh!
Thump.
Swoosh!
Thump.

...were the sounds of the giant taking long strides across the ground. Each step the giant took was about as wide as a baseball field.

Wherever they were going, it was a long way from Uncle Larry's Antique Shop & Junkyard.

5
Magic Tools

Blue sky stretched as far as they could see. Lots of hills were off in the distance, and they were all made of sand.

"Grace, look!" said Eli. "Those are sand dunes."

Behind that, even further away, were a whole bunch of mountains. And the mountains were getting closer with each of the giant's huge, thumping steps.

Swoosh!

Thump.

Swoosh!

Thump.

"I wonder where he's taking us?" asked Grace.

Eli shrugged. He had no clue where the giant was taking them, but the idea of traveling made him think of something else.

"Hey, let's use our magic things," said Eli.

"Good idea," said Grace. She'd been so distracted by the incredible view from the giant's pocket, she nearly forgot about the magic junk Professor Harvard gave them: the bandannas, the bottle cap, and the old postcard.

The first thing they did was pull out the green and white bandannas. Eli tied his around his forehead, then waited for the magic.

"Anything?" he asked.

Grace shook her head. Then she tied her bandanna around her neck.

"Did mine work?" she asked.

Eli shook his head.

No magic happened.

"Try something else," said Eli, then stuffed the bandanna back into his pocket. "All I've got is this old bottle cap."

When Eli pulled the small metal item out of his other pocket, he quickly realized he didn't have a bottle cap anymore. It had changed shape.

He had a compass.

A shiny, brass, antique compass that had to be at least a hundred years old.

"Quick! Check yours," said Eli.

"My postcard?" asked Grace.

"Yes! Hurry!" said Eli. "Maybe we can use them to escape from the giant."

Swoosh!

Thump.

Swoosh!

Thump.

Every second was another giant footstep that took them farther away from Uncle Larry's store, and farther away from Dad.

Grace reached into her back pocket and pulled out her postcard. But the small piece of paper felt much bigger now. It was no longer a faded postcard, but something more detailed.

"Check this out," said Grace, and showed Eli what her magic item had turned into.

A map of the world.

"What's wrong?" asked Eli.

Grace frowned. "Well, it's great that Professor Harvard gave us a compass and a map..."

"Yeah?"

"But there's just one problem..."

"What?"

"How do we get down?" said Grace. "We must be at least a hundred feet in the air!"

Eli peeked over the top of the giant's pocket and looked way down at the ground below.

"More like two hundred feet," said Eli.

Grace had more bad news. "Even if we do somehow get down," she said, "how do we escape? If we run away, the giant will catch us in two seconds."

Now both of them looked worried.

"You're right," said Eli. "I think we need a plan."

The giant showed no sign of slowing down. His wide footsteps covered at least a hundred yards with each step, possibly more once he started jogging.

    Swoosh!

        Thump.

            Swoosh!

                Thump.

Eli and Grace spent the next couple of minutes worrying about what to do. They were both trying to come up with a plan to escape, when the giant suddenly stopped.

From the giant's pocket, all Eli and Grace could see was blue sky, a few clouds, and lots of sandy hills that stretched for miles.

Below them, down on the ground, was some kind of monument. There were flags waving, some benches to sit on, and a big letter "X" going right through the center of the whole thing.

The giant said, "We're here!"

6
Four Corners

The giant reached one hand into his shirt pocket. He carefully scooped up Eli and Grace, then placed them on the ground.

"There you go," said the giant.

"Um, thanks." Eli brushed himself off.

"Yeah, thanks," said Grace.

"I hope the ride wasn't too bumpy," said the giant. "I walk fast even for someone *my* size."

Eli and Grace gazed up at the giant. This was their first chance to get a really good look at him.

The giant had dark skin, glasses, and his hair was long. He wore jeans, a blue button-down shirt, and sneakers like the ones they were wearing.

The only difference was that each of the giant's sneakers was bigger than a used car from Uncle Larry's junkyard.

Grace whispered to her brother that she thought the giant looked like a college professor.

"Are you a teacher?" Eli asked the giant.

"Yes, Eli," said the giant. "I'm a geography teacher. A very large one, but still a normal teacher."

"Oh. That's cool," said Eli. "I love geography and learning about shapes."

The giant's huge eyebrows raised up over the top of his glasses. He looked surprised.

"He said *geography*, Eli," said Grace. "That's when you study places. Geometry is learning about shapes."

The giant smiled. "She's right, my friend. Geometry is the study of shapes, sizes, measurements, lines, angles, and all sorts of fun stuff."

"Oh yeah," said Eli. "I forgot."

"I teach geography," the giant went on. "That

means I know a lot about places. Geography also includes studying things like the climate, and different types of soil and vegetation. I also get to explore different lands, and the inhabitants of those lands."

Grace folded her arms. "See? Told you."

The giant checked his watch.

"Well, guys and gals," said the giant. "That clever old dog told me we don't have a lot of time, but we can still hang out for a little while."

Eli and Grace both looked surprised.

"Did you say...*dog*?" said Eli.

"You mean, Harvard?" asked Grace.

The giant nodded. "Actually, he's Doctor Harvard, but he usually doesn't like it when I call him that," explained the giant. "He used to be my professor. I was his student a long time ago."

Eli was trying to figure it out, while Grace seemed perfectly okay with the idea that Uncle Larry's Golden Retriever was a shape-shifter.

"So, Harvard the dog..." said Eli, trying to wrap his brain around it. "Is Harvard the doctor?"

"Oh, he's more than that, Eli," said the giant. "He's not only a doctor, but he's also a scientist, a physicist, an inventor, an expert in space and time, and about a million other things."

Eli and Grace couldn't believe what they were hearing. Harvard the dog was a genius.

"He helped create all this," said the giant, spreading out his long arms. "Professor Harvard created this world, where kids like you can explore, have fun, and learn."

"Wow," said Eli.

"Yeah," said Grace. "Double wow."

Harvard invented junkyard adventures.

"I'm not sure where Professor Harvard is," said the giant. "But I'm sure we'll run into him at some point." Then he rubbed his big hands together. "Right now, we've got some exploring to do!"

Eli had only one question. "Where are we?"

Grace wondered the same thing. "Yeah, what is this place, Mr. Giant?"

"Oh, you don't have to call me Mr. Giant," said the giant. "That sounds too formal, too stuffy."

"What do we call you?" asked Eli.

"My name is Omar," said the giant.

"Nice to meet you, Omar," said Eli. "So, um, what are we doing here?"

Omar spread out his long arms. "We're here to learn about geography!" he said. "Go on, have a look around. Go check this place out."

Eli and Grace exchanged looks, as if to say, "Why not?" and then headed into the monument.

They walked along the pavement, past a series of benches, a few planted shrubs and trees, and some wheelchair-friendly ramps.

Once they reached the middle, Eli and Grace stood at the center of the marker. The markings were of four states that Eli and Grace had never visited before.

Utah
New Mexico
Colorado
Arizona

"I know what this is!" said Eli. "Omar? Is this the Four Corners place? Where you can be in four different places at the same time?"

Omar smiled down at him. "You got it, Eli!" he said. "This is the famous Four Corners Monument. It's the only point in America where you can stand in four separate states at the same time."

Eli and Grace both took turns standing on the monument, which allowed them to be in four different states all at once. They even lay down on their backs and spread out their arms and legs along the borders of Arizona, Utah, New Mexico, and Colorado.

Flying high above their heads were a bunch of flags. Some flags they knew, but others they weren't sure about.

"Omar?" asked Grace.

"Yes, Grace?"

"What are all those flags?" she asked. "I know the American flag, but what are all the other ones?"

"Great question, Grace," said Omar. "Those

flags represent the four states you two are lying down in. The others are the flags of the Navajo Nation and the Ute Mountain Ute Tribe."

Eli and Grace took a moment to just relax, look into the sky, and think about how cool it was to be in four places at the same time.

"Omar?"

"Yes, Grace?"

"Have you been here before?" asked Grace.

"Oh, sure!" said Omar. "Sometimes I come here on my lunch break, just to sit and think, or look around. Of course, this is the magic version of it, so only the three of us are here."

This gave Eli an idea. "Where else do you go?" he asked, sitting up. "Any other famous places?"

Omar the giant smiled. "Sure, Eli. I've been to famous places all over the world. I'm the Giant of Geography, so I can go anywhere."

"Can we go too?" they both asked.

Omar the giant thought for a moment. He shielded his eyes from the bright sun, then pointed off in the distance.

"Hey, Eli? Do me a favor," said Omar.

"Sure," said Eli. "What is it?"

"Can you check your compass, please?" asked Omar. "Make sure that way is west."

Eli did as he was asked. He checked his compass, and saw that the giant was correct.

"Yeah, you're right," said Eli. "That way is west, but also a tiny bit south."

The giant scratched his chin, thinking.

"Do you two want to go check out one of the world's biggest dams?" asked Omar. He bent all the way down, then held out his hand for them to climb into.

Eli and Grace were lifted back up and placed inside the giant's pocket. This time, nobody fell or crashed on top of each other.

Then, they headed west.

7
Hoover Dam

The Giant of Geography walked from the Four Corners monument to the world famous Hoover Dam in about two minutes.

"Here we are!" said Omar. He allowed his two guests to climb into his hand, then he placed them on the ground so they could look around.

Eli and Grace could see mountains off in the distance, and tall cliffs on either side. Across from where they stood was a brick wall with a big sign.

Hoover Dam
1931 - 1935

When they walked around the corner, Grace was the first one to spot the bridge that stretched from one side of the cliff to another.

"Eli, look!" Grace tapped her brother on the shoulder. "Check out that bridge!"

Eli's eyes grew big. "This place is cool."

Omar agreed. "Yes, Eli, I think geography and learning about new places is very cool."

The Giant of Geography gave them a brief history lesson about the Hoover Dam, and all the work that went into building it.

"Since we're inside the magical junkyard version," explained Omar, "we get to visit this place without the crowd. Unfortunately..."

Omar checked his giant watch.

Eli and Grace knew what he was going to say.

"Time to go?" asked Eli.

"Aww," said Grace. "Time to leave already?"

The Giant of Geography nodded, but he looked disappointed too. "Hey, I'd love to spend all day here with you two," said Omar. "But I think we'd better start heading back. Uncle Larry is doing his best to stall your dad, but soon he'll be ready to leave. But hey, you two can always come back, right?"

"Yeah, we know," they both said.

Visiting famous landmarks and learning about geography was a lot of fun, especially with a great teacher like Omar.

"Just one more?" asked Grace. "Pleeeeease?"

Eli begged too. "What if we go really fast?"

The Giant of Geography fixed his glasses on the end of his nose. He was thinking very hard.

For a moment, Eli and Grace thought the answer would be no. Omar the giant looked very serious. But when he finally made up his mind, he looked down at them, and smiled.

"Oh, all right," said Omar. "We can visit one more famous landmark. But just one, okay?"

Eli and Grace both cheered.

"Have you two ever seen the famous Gateway Arch?" Omar asked them. "It's the tallest man-made monument in the western hemisphere."

Eli and Grace both smiled.

"Nope," they said together.

The Giant of Geography reached down and scooped them up into his hand, then placed them inside his shirt pocket.

"We're nearly out of time," said Omar. "So I'll have to run, okay?"

Eli and Grace told him that was okay with them. They were getting used to traveling this way, inside a giant button-down shirt just like the one's Dad always wore.

"Hey, Eli?" asked Omar. "Can you check your compass one more time, please. I want to make sure we're headed in the right direction. To get to the Gateway Arch, we need to travel northeast."

"Okay, hold on..." Eli pulled out his magic compass, but he had to wait until the pointer arrow settled down. When the arrow finally stopped wiggling around, it was pointed exactly in the direction they were all facing.

"The compass needle is pointing east," said Eli. "East, and a little bit north."

"Good," said Omar. "Oh, and Grace?

"Yes, Omar?"

"If you want, you can follow along on your magic map," said Omar. "It will show the direction from the Arizona and Nevada border, where we are now, all the way to the Gateway Arch."

"Okay, good idea," said Grace. And when she pulled the magic map out of her pocket, there was a bright glowing line that went all the way from the Hoover Dam to St. Louis, Missouri.

"Ready?" asked Omar.

Eli and Grace both said, "Ready!"

"Hold on tight!" said Omar the Giant, as he got ready to run. "Here—we—go!"

Swoosh!

Thump.

Swoosh!

Thump.

8
Gateway Arch

When they arrived in St. Louis, Omar was breathing heavily and his forehead was sweaty. Since they were short on time, he sprinted all the way from the Hoover Dam to St. Louis in only a few minutes. Over 1500 miles!

"Are you okay, Omar?" asked Grace. She was worried that the Giant of Geography had run too fast and injured himself.

"Yeah, I'm fine," said Omar, as he placed Eli and Grace on the ground. "That was a lot...of running. I need to...get more exercise."

Eli and Grace looked around while the Giant of Geography caught his breath.

It didn't take long for them to find the Gateway Arch. All they had to do was walk around the giant's huge feet, then look up.

Eli and Grace couldn't believe their eyes.

The Gateway Arch was a huge steel monument that reached way up high. The Giant of Geography was tall, but this structure was much taller.

"The Arch must be five hundred feet tall!" said Eli excitedly. He had to tilt his neck back so he could see the top of the Arch.

"Actually, Eli, the Gateway Arch is six-hundred and thirty feet tall," said Omar. "The proper name for the Arch is the Jefferson National Expansion Memorial. But most visitors call it the Gateway Arch, or simply The Arch."

The sun gleamed off the steel triangles, adding to the beauty of this famous American monument. Grace wished she had a camera.

"How long did it take to build?" asked Eli.

"A long time, I bet," said Grace.

Omar gave his two new students a brief history of the famous Missouri landmark.

"The Gateway Arch took only two years to build," explained Omar. "There was a contest to see who could come up with the best design."

"Really? Who won?" asked Grace.

"An architect named Eero Saarinen," said Omar. "His design was that the Arch could be built with solid steel triangles. As the Arch gets higher, the steel triangles get smaller."

Omar pointed to a long set of stairs that went all the way down to the entrance.

"Want to ride to the top?" asked Omar.

Eli and Grace both shouted, "Yes!"

After listening to the giant's instructions, the two of them headed down the steps and into the building. Soon they were underneath the Gateway Arch, waiting for an elevator.

After a short ride, Eli and Grace were at the top of the great structure. There were lots of windows to look out, so they had an incredible view of the city of St. Louis.

"You can see the whole city!" said Eli.

"Hey, I see Omar!" said Grace.

More than six hundred feet below, the Giant of Geography was smiling and waving up at them.

Eli and Grace enjoyed the view for a few minutes, able to look in every direction.

"Uh-oh," said Grace, looking down. "I think Omar is trying to tell us something."

When Eli looked down, he saw the Giant of Geography tapping his watch.

"I think we have to go," said Grace.

"Yeah, you're right," said Eli. He didn't want to leave, but he didn't want to miss their ride either. If they didn't have the giant to travel with, they might never get back to Uncle Larry's store.

9
Continents

After another elevator ride, Eli and Grace were back at the bottom of The Arch. They climbed out of the elevator, headed outside, then walked back up the steps to meet the waiting giant.

"I've got some great news," said Omar.

Eli and Grace expected him to say that their adventure was over. Instead, the giant gave them an update about what was happening back at Uncle Larry's store.

"What is it, Omar?" asked Eli.

"Well, your dad is done shopping," explained Omar. "But there are still a few other customers in the store, making their purchases."

"So the store is closed now?" asked Grace.

Omar held up a finger, for silence. Then he put a hand to the side of his head, as he looked off into the distance. Eli and Grace thought he might be checking out the view of the city, or the Mississippi River, which ran right past the Gateway Arch.

"I'm peeking inside Uncle Larry's store right now," explained Omar. "It's just a little junkyard magic that Professor Harvard and Uncle Larry came up with years ago. Oh, hold on..."

Eli and Grace kept quiet while the Giant of Geography used a bit of magic to listen in on the conversation happening back inside the store.

"That's great!" cheered Omar. He clapped his hands, then kneeled down to speak to Eli and Grace, who were wondering what was so exciting.

"What's so great, Omar?" asked Eli.

"Yeah," said Grace. "What happened?"

Omar smiled. "The store just closed, but Uncle Larry and Professor Harvard talked your dad into checking out a used washer and dryer set."

"Really?" said Grace. "You can see all that?"

Omar nodded. "Uncle Larry is just trying to remember where he keeps all the used appliances." He shrugged. "Oh, well. He's got Professor H to help him out."

Eli and Grace were thrilled to hear that their exploring time may have just been extended.

"So, that means...?" Eli grinned.

"We can still explore?" asked Grace.

Omar gave them a thumbs-up.

Eli and Grace slapped each other a hi-five.

"Where should we go?" asked Grace.

The Giant of Geography reached into his jeans pocket and pulled out his own special compass. This compass was bigger than the family SUV, but it fit right into the giant's hand.

"Now *that's* a big compass," said Grace.

Omar laughed. "Professor Harvard invented this compass," he explained. "It's magic! All I have to do is type in the letters, then off we go!"

"Can we really go anywhere?" asked Eli.

"Antarctica?" suggested Grace.

"Sure! We can travel anywhere we want," said Omar. "Just give me a minute to type it in."

ANTARCTICA

The Giant of Geography had a question for his two new students. While he typed in the letters, he gave Eli and Grace a little quiz.

"Do you two know how many continents there are in the world?" asked Omar.

"Seven," said Eli.

"We learned that in school," said Grace.

"That's right," said Omar. "Here's a tricky question. Can you name all seven continents?"

Grace answered first. "There's North America, where we are now. And South America too."

"Asia," said Eli. "Africa."

"Isn't Australia a continent too?" asked Grace. That sounded right, but she wasn't sure if Australia was an island, a continent, or both.

"Yes it is, Grace," said Omar. "Australia is an island *and* a continent. Because it's so big, Australia is called a Continental Island."

Omar finished typing the letters.

They had more exploring to do!

Eli and Grace waited for their ride up to the giant's pocket. But the giant didn't reach down to pick them up.

"Don't we have to ride in your pocket?" asked Eli. By now, they'd both gotten used to it.

"Nope! Not this time," said Omar. "With the push of this magic button, we can travel anywhere in the world."

"Like magic?" asked Grace.

"You got it, Grace," said Omar. "Ready?"

Eli and Grace shouted, "Ready!"

Omar pushed the button, then–

Shhhhhh-ZAP!

With one push of the button, Eli, Grace, and the Giant of Geography traveled through space and time, to arrive in a place with a whole new type of scenery.

Snow and ice.

10
Antarctica

In every direction, snow and ice covered the ground. Great, white hills surrounded them on all sides. Entire mountains made of ice.

As soon as Eli and Grace arrived, they both began to shake because it was cold and windy.

Grace shivered. "It's so cold here."

"It's Antarctica," Eli reminded her. "Of course it's going to be cold."

Grace wrapped her arms around her body to keep warm that way. That didn't work either.

"Here, let's try this..." Omar picked up Eli and Grace. Then he placed them inside his shirt pocket to protect them from the freezing temperature.

"Better?" asked Omar.

"Yes, much better," said Eli.

"Yes," said Grace. "Thank you, Omar."

Not only were they a bit warmer inside the giant's pocket, they were also much higher, so they could see more of Antarctica.

"Eli, look!" said Grace. "The ocean."

"Oh, yeah," said Eli. "I think it's the...hmm."

Grace gave her brother a funny look. "Really? I've never heard of the *hmm* ocean."

"Very funny," said Eli. He thought back to what he'd learned in geography at school. "Antarctica is a continent, and I'm pretty sure it also has its own ocean. This must be the Antarctic Ocean."

"You got it, Eli," said Omar. "We're looking at the Antarctic Ocean, also known as the Southern Ocean. We are more than ten thousand miles from where we were a minute ago, standing at The Gateway Arch back in North America."

The Giant of Geography slowly spun around in a circle. That way, Eli and Grace were able to see everything from his shirt pocket.

"Does anybody live here?" asked Grace.

"Oh, sure!" said Omar, then he pointed toward something off in the distance. There was a series of buildings, some half buried in snow.

"It's only us here right now," said Omar, "but right over there is what we call a station. These stations are where scientists come to work, and study the animals, or learn about climate change. There are quite a few stations down here, which allow people to live in Antarctica all year."

"All year?" asked Eli.

"Sure, Eli!" said Omar. "There's so much to see and explore in Antarctica. And sometimes you get to see a wonderful light show in the sky, just like the Northern Lights."

Grace wondered about something else. She and Eli were still cold, even inside the giant's pocket. But the giant didn't appear to be affected by the low temperature.

"Aren't you cold, Omar?" asked Grace.

Omar took a huge breath. When he exhaled, it produced a great big white cloud.

"No, not really," said Omar. "But I'm a lot bigger, so this temperature feels quite nice to me."

Grace's teeth were chattering.

"Too bad that none of us are dressed for Antarctic weather," said Omar. "Are you two ready to go somewhere a little warmer?"

"Y-y-yes," said Eli and Grace.

"How about South America?" suggested Omar. "We already explored North America, so I'll bet we can find some place warm in, shall we say, Venezuela?"

Eli and Grace both nodded.

"S-s-sounds good..." said Eli.

"Yeah, let's g-g-go," said Grace.

The Giant of Geography typed another location into the magic compass.

VENEZUELA

11
Angel Falls

Faster than they could snap their frozen fingers, all three of them were in a new location. This time they were at the bottom of a great big canyon, with a lush green forest on both sides.

Thankfully, it was warm.

"We're here!" said Omar. He allowed Eli and Grace to jump onto his hand, then he placed them on the rocky ground.

"Grace, look!" said Eli. "Up there!"

Grace drew in a huge breath when she saw where her brother was pointing. She had never seen anything this beautiful before.

A waterfall.

"Welcome to Venezuela," said Omar. "We're standing inside Canaima National Park, directly underneath the world's tallest waterfall, Angel Falls."

Eli and Grace looked up and enjoyed the incredible view. The waterfall went so high that it disappeared into the clouds above. When the water reached the bottom, it turned into a fine mist. Inside the mist were sparkling rainbows that were all carried away by the breeze.

"This is great!" said Eli. "Dad's never taken us to see a waterfall like this before."

Grace jumped to Dad's defense. "Eli, that's because there are no waterfalls like this where we live. We can't all be this close to the world's tallest waterfall."

Omar agreed with Grace. "To travel here, you would have to fly in an airplane. After that, you would have to travel by boat. And since there are no roads to drive on, you would also have to hike a little while through the jungle. But I still think it's worth a visit, don't you?"

"I'll say," said Eli. "The Four Corners Monument was cool. And the Hoover Dam."

"And the Gateway Arch," said Grace.

"Yeah, that too," agreed Eli. "But I've never seen a waterfall so...so..."

"Big?" suggested Grace.

Eli laughed. "Yes, exactly."

Omar was pleased to hear that his two new students were happy, even though both of them still had tiny icicles in their hair.

"Do you want to warm up really fast?" asked Omar. He was already entering a new location.

MOROCCO

"Sure, Omar," said Eli.

"Yes, please," said Grace.

Omar used the magic compass, and they were off once again. This time they were headed to the second largest continent in the world, Africa.

Shhhhhh-ZAP!

12
Africa

One moment Eli and Grace were enjoying the view from Angel Falls, and the next moment they were somewhere new, and very hot.

They were all standing on top of a huge hill, with a long wall about three feet high. The wall was made of sand, just like all the mountains in the distance.

"Welcome to Morocco!" said Omar. "We are now standing in the northwest part of the continent of Africa."

Eli and Grace warmed up quickly. Soon they were starting to sweat a little bit from the heat.

When the two of them walked toward the

edge of the hill and peered over the wall, the view opened up to reveal an entire city.

"Grace, look!" Eli pointed past all the trees, toward a large settlement that was built right into the hill. "It's a whole city!"

The city was unlike anything they'd ever seen before. The buildings and houses were all made of mud and straw, and stood very close together.

"The city is called Ait Benhaddou," said Omar. "It was part of a popular trading route a long time ago. Today it's mostly a place for people to visit."

Eli looked surprised. "Eight...Ben...Who?"

Omar smiled. "It's a tricky one to pronounce, Eli. Instead of its proper name, Ait Benhaddou, lots of people call this place Mud Brick City."

"Does anyone live there?" asked Grace.

"Mud Brick City is mostly a destination for tourists," said Omar. "But yes, a few families do live inside the city."

Eli tried to imagine what it would be like to live in such a city. His sister was thinking about something completely different.

"It sure is hot here," said Grace, and wiped her forehead. "I wish I had on a pair of shorts."

The Giant of Geography allowed Eli and Grace to enjoy the view for another minute. Then he used a bit of junkyard magic to peek into Uncle Larry's store and see what was happening.

"Everything okay, Omar?" asked Eli.

"It looks like your dad isn't quite ready to check out yet," said Omar. "He's still looking over the washer and dryer set with Professor Harvard."

Eli and Grace exchanged excited looks.

"One more continent?" asked Eli.

"Please, Omar?" said Grace.

Omar nodded with a great big smile. "Any preferences?" he asked. "Any requests?"

Eli and Grace both thought about it for a minute, trying to decide where to explore next.

"Hmm," said Eli, thinking. "We've been to North America, South America, and now Africa."

"Don't forget Antarctica," said Grace.

"Oh, yeah, Antarctica too," said Eli. "That means we've visited four of the seven continents."

Omar had a quick question. "Which ones are we missing?" He wiggled his eyebrows. "I'll give you a hint. Two of them start with the letter A."

Eli and Grace knew a couple of answers right away, since the giant had given them a clue.

"Asia," said Eli.

"Australia," said Grace. "We haven't been there yet, either."

"And the last one?" asked Omar, as he peered at them over the top of his giant glasses.

"The last continent is..." Eli scratched his chin.

"The United Kingdom?" suggested Grace. "No, wait. Europe!"

Omar congratulated them both. "Well done!" he said. "If we have time, we'll also visit Europe. But first, let's try somewhere in Asia."

Eli and Grace waited patiently while the giant typed in the letters of a new city.

BUSAN

13
South Korea

With another **click!** of the magic button, they were all transported to a different continent. Mud Brick City magically dissolved, and soon all of them were standing on the continent of Asia.

Eli and Grace could see lots of tall concrete buildings, and some smaller shops nearby. Further on, they could see a great long bridge stretching across the water. There were even mountains right next to the city.

"Now *this* looks like the kind of city we're used to," said Eli. "No mud brick buildings, but still pretty cool."

"Welcome to South Korea," said Omar. "This

is the city of Busan. We are standing inside a popular city park, called Yongdusan Park."

"Yong...doo...san," said Grace, repeating what the giant said.

"Very good, Grace," said Omar. "And up there, behind us, is Busan Tower."

Eli and Grace both turned around and saw a great, white tower with windows at the top.

From where they were standing, the tall tower reached way up into the sky.

"If you two come back," said Omar, "maybe we'll have time to go all the way to the top."

Eli and Grace looked up at Busan Tower.

"How tall is it, Omar?" Eli asked.

"Busan Tower is one hundred and twenty meters tall," Omar told him. "That's nearly four hundred feet."

Eli and Grace loved seeing all these new places, and learning about geography. They always knew the world had many amazing places to explore, but they'd only seen them in pictures.

"Okay, you two," said Omar. "I think we can

squeeze in one more trip. Uncle Larry and Professor Harvard are doing a terrific job of distracting your dad, but they can't stall him forever. Uncle Larry is talking up a storm! And your poor dad is trying his best to pay attention."

Eli and Grace laughed.

Omar checked his watch.

Watching the giant do this, check his watch, it made Grace think about time.

Clocks.

Great big clocks.

"What about Big Ben?" suggested Grace. "Can we go see that big clock in London?"

"Absolutely!" said Omar. Then he had to explain that the famous clock had been renamed.

"It's now called Elizabeth Tower," explained Omar. "Big Ben was renamed after Elizabeth II, for her long reign as Queen."

Omar the giant was already typing the new location into the magic compass.

LONDON

14
Big Clock

When they arrived in London, Eli and Grace had to take a few steps back just so they could see the whole clock tower.

"Does it tell the right time?" asked Grace.

"You bet it does," said Omar. "There are lots of gears, moving parts, and heavy weights that help move the hands of the clock. And the name 'Big Ben' is the nickname for the large bell at the top. When it chimes, you can hear it for miles around."

Eli and Grace took a moment to check out all the old buildings. Most of them didn't look like regular buildings at all, but more like castles.

"I wish Dad were here to see this," said Eli.

Grace agreed. "I'll bet he would like all the neat buildings. They're old, just like him!"

Eli laughed because Dad was always joking about his age, even though he wasn't *that* old.

"London is a lot older than your dad," said Omar. "This city has been around for over two thousand years. And London is also considered one of the great culture capitals of the world."

Ka-bong!

Ka-bong!

Way above their heads, the 30,000-pound bell, Big Ben, began to chime. The noise was so loud that Eli and Grace covered their ears.

The great bell rang six times.

"Uh-oh," said Omar. "It's six o'clock. We need to get back to the junkyard."

Eli was about to say something, but Omar was peeking in on the store again. The giant suddenly cringed when he saw something bad happen.

"Oooh!" said Omar. "That *had* to hurt."

Eli and Grace both looked concerned.

"Is everything okay?" asked Grace.

"Did someone get hurt?" asked Eli.

"Yeah, it's Uncle Larry," said Omar. "He stubbed his toe on a chair. Then a bird cage fell on his head. Right now, he's holding his head and hopping around on one foot."

Eli and Grace wished they could see what the giant saw. They tried hard not to laugh. It's never funny when somebody gets hurt, but they both knew that Uncle Larry was like an accident magnet, since he was always a bit clumsy.

"Your dad is trying to help him out," said Omar, still watching the scene unfold. When he looked back down, he had a huge smile on his face.

"Looks like Uncle Larry can't find the first-aid kit," said Omar. "He's sitting down while your dad goes out to get the one in your vehicle."

Eli and Grace didn't want to get their hopes up, but it sounded like they might have a few more minutes to explore.

"Do we have more time?" asked Grace.

Omar told them the good news. "Looks like we have just enough time to visit the last continent."

Eli grabbed hold of his sister's hand while the Giant of Geography typed one last word into the magic compass.

AUSTRALIA

Omar pushed the button, and all three of them were instantly transported to a new location.

Shhhhhh-ZAP!

But this time, Omar's giant thumb accidentally pushed a button he'd never pressed before.

It was the wrong button.

Eli and Grace went one way, and the Giant of Geography went a different way.

15
Missing Guide

When they arrived this time, Eli and Grace were standing on a sandy beach. A great long beach that looked like it never ended.

In front of them was the South Pacific Ocean.

"This is great!" said Eli. He wanted to take off his socks and shoes and go for a swim.

The smell of the ocean was wonderful. The air was so clean. Small waves came splashing onto the shoreline, not far from where they stood.

When Eli turned around to see what Grace thought about this place, she wasn't smiling at all.

"Eli?" said Grace. "Where's Omar?"

The Giant of Geography was gone.

"I don't see him," said Grace. She scanned the beach, searching for their tall tour guide.

"He must be here somewhere," said Eli, trying not to show his concern. "He's a giant, so he can't be that hard to find."

The bushy green trees behind them had lots of good hiding spots for a human, but not for a giant. If the Giant of Geography was anywhere nearby, they would have seen him.

"Omar!" shouted Eli. "You can come out now!"

They waited, but there was no reply from Omar. When no answer came the second time he shouted Omar's name, Eli took his sister by the hand and they started to walk down the beach.

"Come on, we'll find him," said Eli.

Eli and Grace took turns shouting Omar's name. They called out to the missing giant, over and over, but Omar never answered back.

After walking for quite a while, Eli stopped and turned around. He was surprised to see how far they had walked down the beach.

"I think we should go back," suggested Eli.

"Okay," said Grace. "Then what?"

"And then..." Eli shrugged. "We wait until Omar shows up, I guess. Then we'll go home."

Grace nodded, but Eli could tell she was nervous that something had gone terribly wrong.

"Don't worry," said Eli, trying to comfort his sister. "At least we're still together."

"I miss Dad," said Grace quietly.

Eli squeezed his sister's hand. He wanted to say something comforting to her, like how everything was going to be fine. But that wouldn't be the truth. The truth was that they were in trouble.

Australia was a great place to visit. But they were all alone, on a faraway continent, and their giant guide was missing.

16
Magic Boat

Exploring the world, the continents, and new cities had been wonderful. Eli and Grace never imagined they would get stranded during one of their junkyard adventures.

"Eli, look!" Grace pointed down the beach, back to where they first arrived. "There's a boat."

Where the ocean met the sand, there was an old, broken-down rowboat. It was bobbing side to side in the waves.

As they got closer, they both saw the boat had one of Uncle Larry's price tags on it—$45.00, marked down from $60.00.

"Was it here before?" asked Eli.

Grace shrugged. "I don't know," she said. "But if I still have my magic map, and you still have your magic compass, then..."

Eli caught on quickly. "Then together, we can find our way home. Good thinking, Grace."

"Thanks," said Grace.

With their shoes still on, they splashed into the water and got into the boat. They were feeling much better about completing the adventure.

"Check your map," said Eli. "You tell me which way we need to go, then I'll use my compass to point us in the right direction."

Grace reached into her pocket. Her bright smile disappeared when she pulled out the magic map and showed Eli.

"Oh, great," said Grace. "The magic must've worn off. The map turned back into a postcard."

Eli didn't panic. "That's okay," he said, then reached into his pocket. "We still have the—"

Grace sighed. "Oh, no."

The magic had worn off the compass too. They had a boat, but without a compass or a map, they had no idea which direction they needed to travel. If they started paddling the wrong way, there was no telling where they would end up.

"Hey, wait a second—" Grace flipped over the postcard and saw a bunch of writing. "There's a note scribbled on the back. It's from Omar!"

Grace read the note out loud.

Eli & Grace,

If something goes wrong or we get separated somehow, use the boat to get back home.
Omar

PS — This is a magic boat. Just tell it nicely where you want to go, and it will take you there.

"Well, sis? There's our answer," said Eli. "Looks like we're taking a long boat ride to get back."

Speaking directly to the boat, Eli cupped his hands and took a really deep breath.

"BOAT!" shouted Eli. "Take us that way!" He pointed southeast, which was way off course.

The boat didn't move.

"Hm," said Eli, stumped. "I guess the magic has worn off this old boat too."

Grace shook her head. "Omar's note said you have to tell the boat *nicely*," she reminded him. "Try it again. But be polite this time. And you should probably ask the boat to take us back to Uncle Larry's Antique Shop and Junkyard."

"Oh. Right," said Eli, looking a little bit embarrassed. "Good thinking."

In a much softer voice, Eli said, "Excuse me, Mr. Boat? Could you take us back to Uncle Larry's Antique Shop and Junkyard?"

Grace coughed to get Eli's attention.

"*Please*," Eli said to the boat.

The boat did as it was told.

"See?" said Grace. "Just be polite."

With a little junkyard magic, the oars started to row themselves. Very slowly at first, but then the boat picked up speed. Soon the sandy beach was no longer visible. Their tiny rowboat, just big enough for two, was headed across the ocean.

17
The Pilot

Eli was beginning to feel a bit nervous about their plan. At this speed, their boat ride could last several days. Thankfully, Grace was the first one to spot something way up in the sky.

A plane flew overhead.

"What's an airplane doing in our junkyard adventure?" wondered Grace. "It's really close."

Eli shielded his eyes from the sun. He noticed right away that the plane didn't have wheels. Instead, there were what looked like two kayak boats stuck on the bottom.

"It's a seaplane!" said Eli, as they watched the large vessel land right on top of the water.

Once the plane came to a stop, the pilot opened a large door and waved at them.

It was Professor Harvard.

"Great work, you two!" said Professor Harvard. "Sometimes these junkyard adventures can take an unexpected turn. When that happens, you have to improvise a little bit. And you both did an excellent job!"

"Thanks, Professor," said Eli. Then he asked, "Is this your plane? Are you really a pilot?"

"Did you use magic?"

"Have you seen Omar?"

"Is Dad mad at us?"

Professor Harvard held up his hand. "I know you must have a lot of questions, but we need to get you two back. This junkyard adventure went on longer than expected."

It was time for one last stop. And that would be Uncle Larry's Antique Shop & Junkyard.

Once everyone was safely inside the seaplane, Eli and Grace got buckled up while Professor Harvard prepared for takeoff.

"Professor, we traveled all over the world!" said Eli, as he tightened his seatbelt.

"To all seven continents!" said Grace, as she buckled hers too.

"Yes, I know," said Professor Harvard. "I've been keeping track of you from the store."

Professor Harvard turned on the engines.

"When Omar showed up at the junkyard without you..." said Professor Harvard. "Well, that's when I knew something went wrong. I had to act quickly. I left your dad with Uncle Larry. Then I hurried off to find you."

The plane was skimming across the water.

"What did happen, Professor?" asked Grace.

"Did Omar push the wrong button?" asked Eli.

"That's part of it," said Professor Harvard. "But it was also *my* fault."

"Your fault?" said Grace.

"I must have pushed the button on my compass at the same time Omar pushed his button," explained Professor Harvard.

From the pilot's seat, Professor Harvard held

out his hairy arm for them to see. Instead of a wristwatch, Professor Harvard wore a magic compass. It was the exact same magic compass that Omar had, only smaller.

"And then..." Professor Harvard shrugged. "Omar was transported back to the junkyard, and you two were sent halfway around the world."

"Yeah, all the way to Australia," said Eli.

"The beach was nice," said Grace. "But it was kind of scary when Omar didn't show up."

"That's why I brought the seaplane," explained Professor Harvard. "As a backup, just in case the magic compass needs to be repaired."

They were already in the air. This was the first time Eli and Grace had ever been on a plane—or *seaplane*. The ride was smooth, but it was still a little bit scary, since they'd never flown before.

Professor Harvard had everything set properly, and they were ready to go. "Are you two ready to go back to the junkyard? Back home?"

"Ready!" said Eli and Grace.

Once they were safely at 10,000 feet, Professor

Harvard dialed in the letters on his magic wristwatch compass. He gave Eli and Grace a quick warning, then pushed the button next to the words:

UNCLE LARRY'S JUNKYARD

And just like that—

Shhhhhh-ZAP!

—they were back at Uncle Larry's store.

But their troubles weren't over yet.

"Okay, Eli and Grace!" said Professor Harvard. "It's safe to unbuckle now. But you two have one more thing to do..."

Eli and Grace undid their seat belts, then stood up and walked toward the cockpit.

"If you look out the little round windows," said Professor Harvard, "you can see that we're still inside the junkyard adventure. That means you will need to reach the junkyard door before your dad does."

Eli and Grace both agreed.

"What will happen if we don't?" asked Eli.

"Yeah," said Grace. "What if Dad gets there first? We'll probably be grounded forever if he finds out we traveled the whole world."

Professor Harvard looked thoughtful for a minute as he considered this.

"I'm not exactly sure what would happen," said Professor Harvard. "In all these years of adventures, kids have always returned on time. And always before any grownups discover the magic of the junkyard."

Professor Harvard steered the plane left, going around in a huge circle above the junkyard.

"Then we better land quickly," said Eli.

"Yeah, before Dad gets there," said Grace.

"Where do we land, Professor?" asked Eli. "Is there enough room down there to land?"

Professor Harvard was quiet for so long that Eli and Grace knew something was up.

"Well, here's the deal," said Professor Harvard. "This seaplane was built as an amphibious craft."

"Am-phib-i-ous," said Grace, thinking hard. "That means land and water, right?"

"Correct, Grace," said Professor Harvard. "This plane can land on any type of surface. Unfortunately, we're out of time. That means you two will have to jump."

Eli and Grace thought they'd heard wrong.

"We have to...*jump*?" Eli looked over at his sister. She was in shock too.

Grace's heart immediately began to thump at the idea of jumping out of a plane.

"Put on your parachutes," said Professor Harvard. "You'll be fine!"

"But we don't have—" Eli began to say, but then he stopped. He already knew the answer.

"Check your pockets," said Professor Harvard. "Those magic handkerchiefs I let you borrow will work quite nicely. I invented them myself."

As soon as Eli and Grace reached into their pockets and pulled out their handkerchiefs—

Thump!

Two heavy sacks hit the floor of the plane.

Parachutes.

18
Skydive

Professor Harvard had to circle the seaplane around the junkyard a second time. They missed their first chance because Eli refused to skydive.

"Quickly, Eli! Hurry, Grace!" said Professor Harvard from the cockpit. "Your dad is headed for the back door! He's calling for you! You two need to get back before he reaches the junkyard!"

The side door of the plane was open. The wind rushed past. They were all set to jump, but 10,000 feet separated them from the junkyard.

Eli was shaking his head.

"Forget it!" said Eli. His backpack was all strapped and secured, but he wouldn't jump.

"I am *not* jumping out of an airplane," said Eli.

"Seaplane," Grace reminded him.

"Whatever!" shouted Eli. "I am not jumping out of any kind of plane."

Grace knew her brother got nervous and scared sometimes. Especially with heights.

"Eli? We don't have a choice," said Grace. "We've already come this far, so please don't get scared now."

"I'm not scared," said Eli, though it was easy to tell that he was.

Grace quickly put on her parachute. She hoisted it over her shoulders and locked all the buckles. It was just like putting on her backpack for school, but with a few extra buckles.

"I'm going to circle around one last time," said Professor Harvard. "Then you'll have to jump."

Grace could tell that Eli wouldn't budge. Seeing the terrified look on her brother's face, she grabbed hold of Eli's hand, and then looked him right in the eyes when she spoke.

"We'll be fine, Eli," said Grace. "I promise."

Eli smiled, but only a little. He took a deep breath and looked out the door again, trying not to panic or think about the ground down below.

"Fine, I'll do it," said Eli. Then he shuffled his feet toward the door, and waited for instructions.

"Okay," asked Eli. "Now what?"

"Now, you jump!" said Professor Harvard. "You'll do great, Eli! You too, Grace!"

All the rushing wind made it difficult to hear, but they were pretty sure they heard Professor Harvard say something about the landing. And he also shouted something about Omar, which they didn't quite understand.

Eli wished there was a better option. He wished they had just a little more time to come up with a different plan.

Grace had her own plan.

"On three, okay?" Eli was breathing heavily and looked very pale.

"Okay, on three," agreed Grace.

"One..." said Eli.

"Two..." said Grace.

"Ahhhhhhhhhhh!"

Eli was suddenly flying through the air. He was dropping from the sky at a rate of nearly two hundred feet per second.

Grace knew he wouldn't go on his own. That's why she had decided that the best way to get him out of the plane would be...to *push* him.

"Bye, Professor Harvard!" said Grace.

"Bye, Grace!" said Professor Harvard. "I'll see you back in the junkyard!"

Grace took a big breath, then jumped.

19
Handy Landing

Everything happened so fast that Eli and Grace didn't feel scared anymore. The moment they jumped from Professor Harvard's seaplane, the nervous feeling for both of them disappeared, and they were soon having fun.

"This is great!" shouted Eli. He wasn't sure if Grace heard him or not because of the noisy wind, but she was laughing and smiling.

Grace gave her brother a thumbs-up.

Neither of them had parachuted before, so they didn't understand how a parachute works. Only after they had jumped did they realize that their bandanna-parachutes didn't have a ripcord like a regular parachute. Which, they would soon find out, wasn't a problem when wearing a magic parachute from Uncle Larry's.

At the proper time, and not a second before, their parachutes opened all on their own. Eli and Grace didn't have to do a thing. The magic parachutes were easy to control.

"That was amazing!" said Grace, as she drifted down next to her brother's parachute.

"I know!" said Eli. "There's the junkyard! I'll bet we can aim right for the middle of it!"

Looking down, they suddenly realized that the ground was getting much closer. Which raised an extremely important question, as the two of them continued to drop from the sky.

How were they going to land?

Luckily, a giant was there to help.

"It's Omar!" shouted Eli.

"I see him!" Grace shouted back.

Eli and Grace used the control toggles to guide their parachutes, steering left and right. They were trying to aim right for Omar's hand.

"You're doing great!" shouted Omar. "Just a little bit further...there you go...that's it..."

Eli floated down, down, down.

"A little more..."

Thump.

"Welcome back!" said Omar. He caught Eli in the palm of his great big hand. "Great job, Eli."

"Thanks, Omar!" Eli had never felt so relieved. He wanted to kiss the ground just as soon as Omar placed him on the solid earth.

Grace wasn't far behind.

"That's it, Grace!" Omar kept his giant hand directly beneath her. "Just a little bit more..."

Thump.

"We made it!" cried Grace. She landed perfectly in Omar's hand, and he lowered her to the ground. She was relieved to see that the Giant of Geography had also made it back safely.

"Are you okay, Omar?" asked Grace. "We were worried about you. We thought we lost you."

Omar nodded. "Yes, I'm fine. I'm just glad that you two are safe. I was so worried when you and

Eli went one way, and I went another way."

Grace waved it off like it was no big deal. "We found your note!" she said. "Then we worked together and came up with a plan."

"Great!" said Omar. "How was Australia?"

"Well?" said Grace. "The beach was nice."

"The whole junkyard adventure was great!" said Eli, though he was glad to be back. He was going to tell Omar more, but he was interrupted.

Someone was shouting.

It was Dad.

"Eli? Grace?" said Dad. "Where are you? It's time to go! Uncle Larry is closing up the store."

Omar waved at them to go. "You can tell me all about it later," he whispered. "Get back inside the store! Hurry!"

As fast as they could, Eli and Grace ran toward the door with the familiar sign.

JUNKYARD ADVENTURES

20
Washer & Dryer

Eli and Grace got there just in time to stop their dad from entering the junkyard. If they had been too late, then their dad might have seen the Giant of Geography standing there, waving down at them from way up high. Then who knows what would have happened.

"Hi, guys," said Dad. "Where were you? I've been calling for you. I was starting to get worried."

Eli and Grace both hugged their dad, squeezing him tight. Dad loved hugs, but this reaction surprised him.

"Is everything okay?" asked Dad.

Eli and Grace squeezed him even harder.

"I've only been gone a few minutes," said Dad, soaking up the attention. "You two are acting like you haven't seen me in days!"

Swoosh!
Thump.
Swoosh!
Thump.

A loud noise came from somewhere out in the junkyard. It sounded like the gravel and rocks crunching underneath a large pair of shoes.

"What was that noise?" Dad looked out the door, checking the junkyard for a long time. If he had looked hard enough, he might have seen a large shoe slip out of sight behind a used car.

"Oh, probably nothing, Dad," said Eli, trying to think of a distraction. "Maybe...the wind?"

"Or Professor Harvard, in his human form?" said Grace, then quickly realized her mistake. "I mean, Harvard the dog in his, um...dog form."

Dad gave them a curious look.

"No, Harvard is right there," said Dad, then

pointed back inside the store. Uncle Larry and his trusted old guard dog were walking down the aisle, heading toward them.

Professor Harvard had returned to the shape of a big, scruffy Golden Retriever. His tongue was sticking out and his tail was wagging.

Eli and Grace waved at him.

Harvard barked happily.

"Oh, well." Dad shrugged. "Must've been my imagination, I guess..."

Eli and Grace were relieved when Dad gave up the search and went back inside the store.

It was time to head home.

Uncle Larry walked them out to the car and helped them load all their new decorations for the aquarium.

Harvard came too. The friendly dog jumped right up into the SUV while Eli and Grace were getting buckled up in the back seat.

When everyone was all set, Harvard jumped back out and stood next to Uncle Larry.

"Bye, Harvard!" said Eli.

"Bye, Uncle Larry!" said Grace.

Dad started the car, then everybody waved goodbye to Uncle Larry and Harvard.

"Bye, Eli! Bye, Grace!" shouted Uncle Larry. "See you soon, Bernard!"

Dad laughed when Uncle Larry said his name wrong—*again*.

"See you soon, Larry!" called Dad.

Eli and Grace exchanged curious looks in the back seat. It sounded like Dad had already made plans to come back and visit Uncle Larry's Antique Shop & Junkyard.

Dad pulled out onto Broadway Street. After driving through the busy downtown traffic, they were on their way home.

"Dad?"

"Yes, Grace?"

"Can we stop for ice cream?" she asked.

"Not today," said Dad, as they drove along. "We kept Uncle Larry working until after six o'clock. You guys must be hungry. Let's go home."

"Okay, Dad," they both said.

Eli and Grace weren't upset, especially since they'd just had an amazing adventure. They traveled all around the world, and got to visit the seven continents with their new friend Omar, the Giant of Geography.

Eli and Grace couldn't help but wonder when they might have their next junkyard adventure.

"Besides..." said Dad. "While you two were choosing your decorations for the aquarium, I was speaking to Uncle Larry's friend, that Professor."

"You were?" asked Eli, sounding hopeful.

"And?" said Grace with a smile.

"*And*..." said Dad, as they turned right and headed down their street. "I may have put a down payment on a used washer and dryer set. But I told Uncle Larry that I couldn't pick it up until next week."

In the back seat, Eli and Grace smiled at each other. They knew just what to ask.

"Can we go too?"

GIANT of GEOGRAPHY

Follow the Junkyard Adventure!

Eli and Grace traveled the world with the Giant of Geography. Use the map below to see where they went! And to learn more about the seven continents.

(in order of appearance in the book)

1) North America

2) Antarctica

3) South America

4) Africa

5) Asia

6) Europe

7) Australia

1
North America

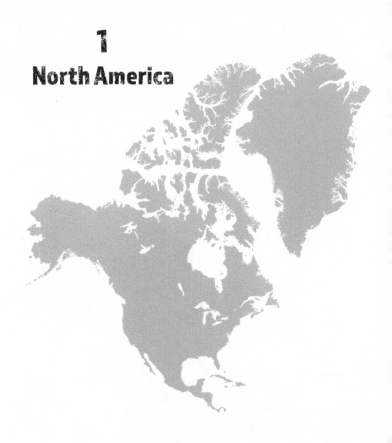

Did you know...

1) North America is the third largest continent.
2) North America is made up of 23 countries.
3) North America's largest city is Mexico City, in Mexico.

 Fun Fact:

Lake Superior (located in Michigan) is the largest freshwater lake in the world.

2
Antarctica

Did you know...

1) Antarctica is the fifth largest continent.
2) Antarctica is called a "polar desert."
3) 98% of Antarctica is covered in ice.

 Fun Fact:

Antarctica was the last region on Earth to be discovered, back in the year 1820.

3
South America

Did you know...

1) South America is the fourth largest continent.
2) South America is made up of 12 countries.
3) South America's largest city is Sao Paulo, in Brazil.

 **Fun Fact:**

South America is home to the largest rainforest in the world, the Amazon Rainforest. Over two million square miles!

4
Africa

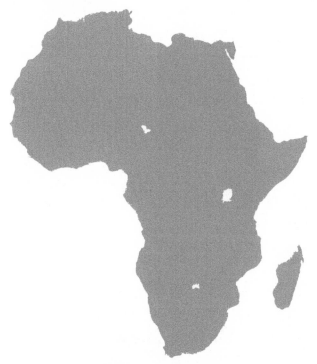

Did you know...

1) Africa is the second largest continent.
2) Africa is currently made up of 54 countries.
3) Africa's largest city is Lagos, in Nigeria.

 **Fun Fact:**

Africa is home to the Nile River, the longest river in the world. The Nile River is over 4,130 miles long!

105

5
Asia

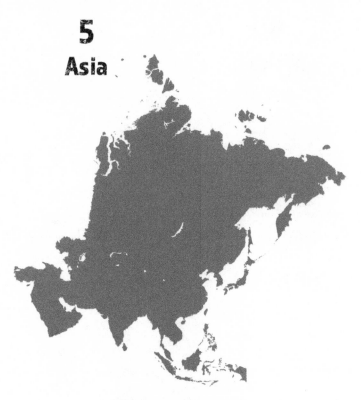

Did you know...

1) Asia is the largest continent in the world.
2) Asia is currently made up of 48 countries.
3) Asia's largest city is Tokyo, in Japan.

 **Fun Fact:**

Asia is such a big place that it makes up over 30% of the land on Earth. It also has the highest point on Earth's surface, the tip-top of Mount Everest.

6
Europe

Did you know...

1) Europe is the sixth largest continent in the world.
2) Europe is currently made up of 50 countries.
3) Europe's largest city is London, in England.

 **Fun Fact:**

Europe is home to the city of Olympia, located in Greece, where great competitions were held. Centuries later, we still have the Olympic Games.

7
Australia

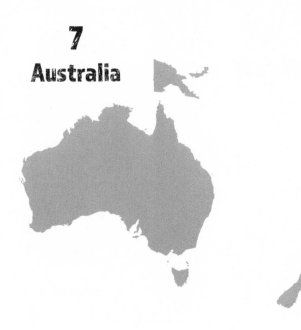

Did you know...

1) Australia is the smallest continent in the world.
2) Australia is the only continent that's also a country.
3) Australia's largest city is Sydney.

 Fun Fact:

Australia is home to the Great Barrier Reef, the largest coral reef in the world. (The "GBR" was the inspiration for Eli and Grace's underwater adventure in *Sea Serpent of Science*, Junkyard Adventure Book #2.)

About the Author

Tevin Hansen is the multi-award-winning author of more than 20 middle grade books, including *Hole in the Wall*, *Hairytale Adventures*, and the *Junkyard Adventures* series. He enjoys writing fast-paced, humorous books for kids, and also the occasional YA novel. Tevin lives in Lincoln, Nebraska, with his wife, kids, and a collection of cheap guitars.

Leave an Amazon review...

...get a free poster!

Help us reach our goal of 100+ reviews per book.

Visit **www.TevinHansen.com** for more information.

What constellation will you find with the Alien of Astronomy?

A JUNKYARD ADVENTURE

Alien of ASTRONOMY

TEVIN HANSEN

A JUNKYARD ADVENTURE

Mermaid of MUSIC

Music Crafts Inside

TEVIN HANSEN

Make a beautiful melody with the Mermaid of Music.

A JUNKYARD ADVENTURE

ART MONSTER

CRAFT PROJECTS INSIDE

TEVIN HANSEN

Get creative with the Art Monster.

Hairytale Adventures

Read all three Alexia & Melvin chapter books!

Alexia and Melvin have a complicated relationship. And that mean old bear doesn't make things any easier.

Made in the USA
Las Vegas, NV
02 August 2022

52567662R00069